THE ULTIMATE INTERACTIVE GUIDE TO
NATURAL DISASTERS

CONTENTS

EARTH FACT FILE

Diameter	7,926 miles
Atmosphere	78% nitrogen 21% oxygen 1% other gases
Average temperature	59°F
Number of moons	1
Distance from Sun	93 million miles
Length of year	365.25 days
Length of day	24 hours

Volcanoes

Earth is a planet in motion. Even the ground under your feet moves. It's usually so slow that you don't notice it, but natural disasters like volcanoes and earthquakes cause more sudden movements.

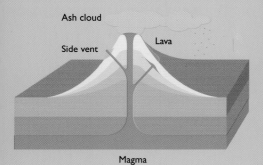

Ash cloud

Side vent

Lava

Magma

Natural disasters and extreme weather are the most violent and dangerous events in nature. Earth is a very active planet. In some places the ground may suddenly shift and shake in a shattering earthquake. Volcanoes might erupt and spew out lava and ash. The air that surrounds the Earth is in motion all the time too. The weather is usually calm, but nature can make some very wild weather. It can create giant storms and floods. It can whip up winds as fast as an express train and send dazzling lightning flashes across the sky. There are even dangers that come from outer space.

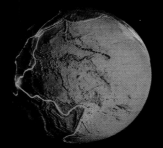 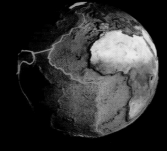

A cracked Earth

Earth is like a giant egg with a cracked shell. The thin crust of rock that forms its surface is broken into pieces called tectonic plates. These plates move slowly and their edges grind against each other. Earthquakes and volcanoes are common in these places.

The water cycle

Water is continually moving between the oceans, the atmosphere, and the land. This is called the water cycle. Water evaporates from the land and oceans. It is carried aloft by rising air currents and it may travel long distances before it falls back to the surface again as rain or snow.

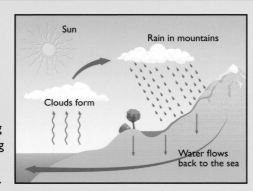

Sun

Rain in mountains

Clouds form

Water flows back to the sea

Equator

The Sun's rays are more concentrated at the equator.

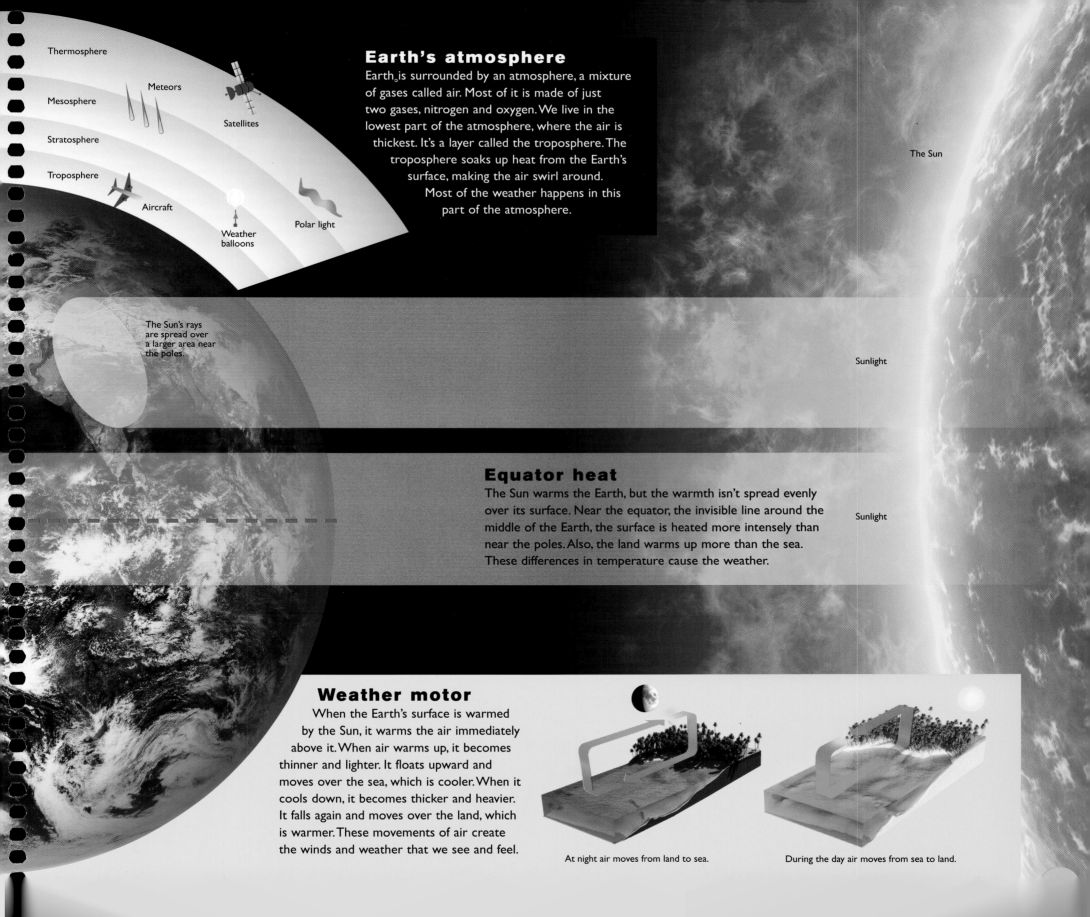

Thermosphere

Mesosphere

Stratosphere

Troposphere

Meteors

Satellites

Aircraft

Weather balloons

Polar light

Earth's atmosphere

Earth is surrounded by an atmosphere, a mixture of gases called air. Most of it is made of just two gases, nitrogen and oxygen. We live in the lowest part of the atmosphere, where the air is thickest. It's a layer called the troposphere. The troposphere soaks up heat from the Earth's surface, making the air swirl around. Most of the weather happens in this part of the atmosphere.

The Sun

The Sun's rays are spread over a larger area near the poles.

Sunlight

Equator heat

The Sun warms the Earth, but the warmth isn't spread evenly over its surface. Near the equator, the invisible line around the middle of the Earth, the surface is heated more intensely than near the poles. Also, the land warms up more than the sea. These differences in temperature cause the weather.

Sunlight

Weather motor

When the Earth's surface is warmed by the Sun, it warms the air immediately above it. When air warms up, it becomes thinner and lighter. It floats upward and moves over the sea, which is cooler. When it cools down, it becomes thicker and heavier. It falls again and moves over the land, which is warmer. These movements of air create the winds and weather that we see and feel.

At night air moves from land to sea.

During the day air moves from sea to land.

Number of thunderstorms worldwide each year	16 million
Number of thunderstorms at any moment worldwide	18,000
Diameter of a typical thunderstorm	15 miles
Lifetime of a typical thunderstorm	30 minutes
Place that suffers the most thunderstorms	Kampala, Uganda
Temperature of a lightning bolt	54,000°F
Length of a typical lightning bolt	5 miles
Number of people killed by lightning every year	About 2,000

Microburst

Thunderstorms can produce an effect called a microburst that is very dangerous to aircraft. A strong wind may suddenly blow straight down from the bottom of a thunderstorm. It can be powerful enough to knock over trees or crash a low-flying aircraft. Large airports now have detectors that warn of microbursts.

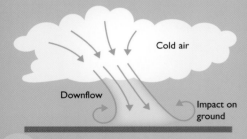

Cold air

Downflow

Impact on ground

THUNDER AND LIGHTNING

A thunderstorm is one of nature's most awesome events. A giant dark cloud grows taller and taller until it towers up to 10 miles over the ground. Then it lets loose a torrent of rain and sometimes hailstones. The wind gusts faster and faster. Inside the cloud, electric charges build up until flashes of lightning streak across the sky, sending out claps of thunder. It's not a good idea to fly through a thundercloud. Airplanes avoid them. When the *Apollo 12* spacecraft was launched in 1969 on its way to the Moon with three astronauts inside, it was struck by lightning. Luckily, the spacecraft and its rocket were not damaged.

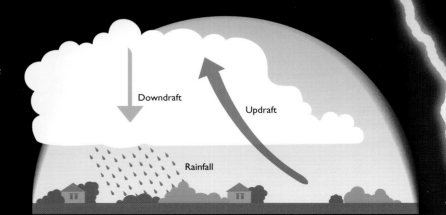

Downdraft

Updraft

Rainfall

How storms form

Air currents carry water droplets upward inside a thundercloud. They grow bigger and some of them fall as rain. Others are carried up and down again and again. They freeze and grow bigger as more water freezes onto them, forming large hailstones.

Giant waves

A big storm has the ability to raise the sea level. Low air pressure in the storm sucks the sea upward, like sucking water up a straw. If this happens at the same time as a high tide, the storm may blow the raised sea onto a coastline and cause serious flooding. This is called a storm surge.

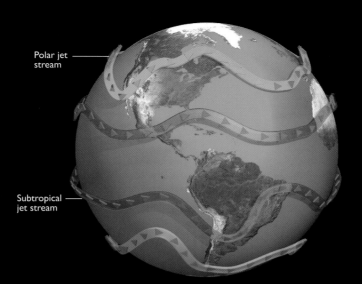

Polar jet stream

Subtropical jet stream

Jet streams

Strong winds called jet streams blow around the world high above the ground. They mark places where warm air from the tropics meets cold air from the poles. They can make storms below them more intense. Jet stream winds can reach speeds of up to 200 mph.

Lightning strikes

Towers and skyscrapers are often struck by lightning. Tall structures like this are protected by lightning conductors. A lightning conductor is a thick metal rod or strap that goes from the top of the structure all the way down to the bottom. It leads lightning safely down into the ground.

Mighty thunder

Lightning is nature's own fireworks display. Each flash is a spark of electricity. A small spark makes a clicking noise, but a flash of lightning makes a loud bang that we hear as thunder. Most lightning never reaches the ground. It flashes inside clouds or from one cloud to another.

Fulgurite glass

When a bolt of lightning hits the ground, it can start fires, blow trees apart, cause power cuts, and sometimes even turn the ground to glass! When lightning strikes sandy ground, the intense heat it produces melts the sand and changes it into glass. It forms a glass rod or tube called a fulgurite. A fulgurite is a bolt of lightning made solid.

Windiest continent	Antarctica
The fastest wind ever recorded	301 mph inside a tornado in Oklahoma City on May 3, 1999
The fastest wind outside a tornado	253 mph on April 10, 1996, on Barrow Island off the northwest coast of Australia during Cyclone Olivia
The fastest wind outside a tornado or tropical cyclone	231 mph on Mount Washington, New Hampshire, on April 12, 1934
The fastest average daily wind speed	108 mph at Port Martin, Antarctica, on March 21–22, 1951

Airships

The top of the Empire State Building was designed as a mooring mast for airships. However, it proved to be too dangerous for airships because of strong winds blowing up the building from the street below.

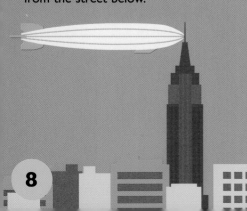

WILD WIND

Wind is simply moving air. It's hard to believe that a thin gas you can't even see could do more than rustle a few leaves. But wind is no weakling. If it blows fast enough, it has enormous power. It can uproot trees or destroy buildings. It starts causing damage when it reaches a speed of about 50–60 mph. Half of all the weather damage in the lower 48 U.S. states is caused by wind. The most extreme winds on Earth can reach speeds of more than 200 mph. Luckily, wind as fast as this is very rare.

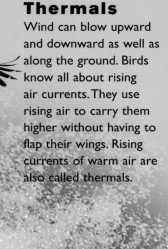

Thermals

Wind can blow upward and downward as well as along the ground. Birds know all about rising air currents. They use rising air to carry them higher without having to flap their wings. Rising currents of warm air are also called thermals.

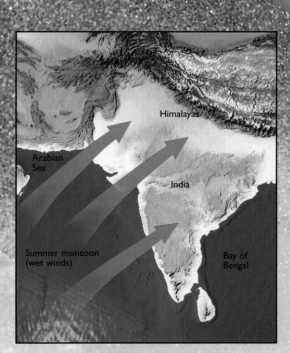

Himalayas

Arabian Sea

India

Summer monsoon (wet winds)

Bay of Bengal

Monsoon winds

When air rises over hot land, more air is sucked in from the sea to replace it. In some parts of the world, especially in India, the land gets so hot every summer that the winds blowing in from the sea return every year. In the winter, the winds reverse and blow in the opposite direction, from the land to the sea. They're called monsoon winds.

Beaufort number	Wind speed (mph)	Nautical term		Effect on land
0	Under 1	Calm		Smoke rises vertically
1	1–3	Light air		Smoke drifts
2	4–7	Light breeze		Leaves rustle
3	8–12	Gentle breeze		Flags move
4	13–18	Moderate breeze		Small branches move
5	19–24	Fresh breeze		Small trees sway
6	25–31	Strong breeze		Large branches move
7	32–38	Moderate gale		Difficult to walk
8	39–46	Fresh gale		Small branches break off
9	47–54	Strong gale		Slates blown off roof
10	55–63	Whole gale		Trees blown down
11	64–72	Storm		Widespread damage
12	73 or higher	Hurricane force		Serious destruction

Beaufort scale

You might hear a wind described as gale force 8 or storm force 11. The numbers show how fast the wind is blowing. They belong to a scale invented in 1805 by a British Royal Navy officer, Sir Francis Beaufort. He invented it so that all naval officers on ships would record wind speeds in the same way.

Gliding

Glider and hang glider pilots use rising air currents, including thermals, to keep them up in the air for longer. They can tell where the rising air currents are from the shape of the ground, the weather, and by watching birds.

Mountain gales

Near the ground, wind is slowed down by hills, trees, and buildings, but higher up there is nothing to slow it. Gales can be dangerous to mountain climbers. If they see snow blowing off a mountaintop, it may be too windy to climb.

Strong winds

Blown snow

Mountain

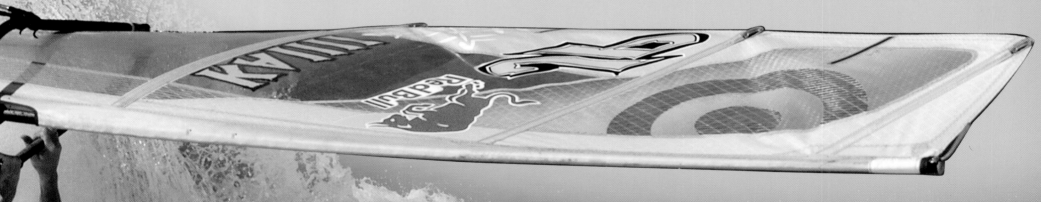

Windsurfing

When wind blows over water, it produces waves on the water's surface. Waves can be as small as ripples or as much as 100 feet high. The biggest waves are made by hurricanes. They can travel across an ocean before they break on a seashore. Surfers and windsurfers enjoy these wind-blown waves.

Windy city

Skyscrapers change the way wind blows through a city. When the first skyscrapers were built, people noticed that the streets were windier. The buildings were causing the high winds. Nowadays, models of new buildings are tested to check how the buildings will affect the wind.

9

Storm size	Typically 280–400 miles across
Eye size	2–200 miles across
Spin direction	Clockwise in the Southern Hemisphere, counterclockwise in the Northern Hemisphere
Speed across ground	Up to 20 mph
Lifetime	7–10 days
Biggest Atlantic hurricane	Hurricane Sandy (2012), 1,100 miles across
Biggest Pacific typhoon	Typhoon Tip (1979), 1,380 miles across
Highest wind speed	Typhoon Haiyan (2013), 195 mph
Costliest Atlantic hurricane	Hurricane Katrina ($125 billion)
Hurricane deaths	2 million over the past 200 years

Bangladesh

Some of the world's deadliest tropical cyclones form in the Bay of Bengal, to the east of India. The low-lying islands and coasts of Bangladesh to the north are especially at risk from flooding caused by storm surges. Some of the worst cyclones ever recorded have caused great loss of life there.

Bangladesh

India

Bay of Bengal

10

SUPERSTORMS

The most extreme storms are hurricanes. They are also called cyclones and typhoons depending on where they are. These are massive rotating storms with a clear hole in the middle called the eye. Warm water is the secret of their huge size and power. Warm ocean water in the tropics supplies the energy they need to form and grow. A hurricane travels across the ocean, growing bigger and more powerful. Its high-speed winds, torrential rain, and storm surge flooding can do a lot of damage to the islands and coasts it passes over. When it crosses a coastline onto the land, its supply of warm, moist air from the ocean is cut off and it quickly fades away.

Storm regions

Hurricanes are known by different names in different places. They're called hurricanes in the western Atlantic Ocean and eastern Pacific Ocean. In the northwest Pacific Ocean, they're called typhoons. In the Indian Ocean, the Bay of Bengal, and near Australia, they're called cyclones. If a hurricane crosses from one side of the Pacific Ocean to the other, it becomes a typhoon.

Category	Winds (mph)	Damage
1	74–95	Minimal
2	96–110	Moderate
3	111–130	Major
4	131–155	Extensive
5	155 and more	Catastrophic

Hurricane strength

A hurricane's strength is given by its category number. The category scale goes from category 1 to category 5. Category 5 hurricanes are the most powerful and dangerous. They have wind speeds of more than 155 mph and they can cause terrible destruction over a wide area.

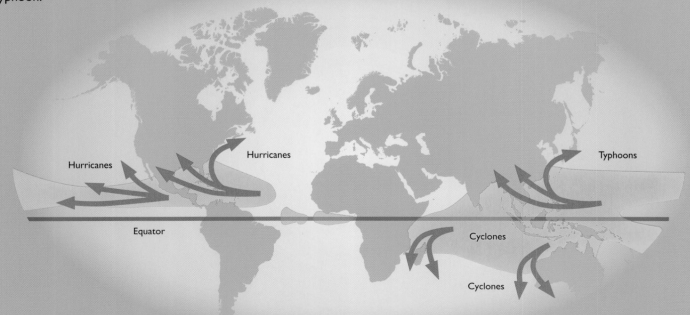

Hurricanes

Hurricanes

Typhoons

Cyclones

Cyclones

Equator

Eye

Cool falling air

Eye wall

Warm rising air

Rain bands

Low pressure

Naming storms

Typhoon Haiyan, which devastated the Philippines in 2013, was one of the strongest tropical cyclones ever recorded. These giant storms are given names because there can be more than one at a time. Giving each storm a different name makes it clear which storm weather forecasters are talking about.

Inside a hurricane

Warm, moist air at the bottom of a hurricane spirals in toward the center. When it reaches the eye at the center of the hurricane, it spirals up the eye wall. The wind is at its fastest here. When it reaches the top of the eye, it spills outward. More air is sucked in at the bottom of the hurricane and up through the eye to replace the rising air. This fast-moving core is surrounded by bands of thunderclouds and rain.

The view from space

Hurricane Dennis, a category 4 storm, swept across the Gulf of Mexico toward the coast of Florida in 2005. Astronauts and satellites in space get the best views of superstorms like Hurricane Dennis. Looking down from above, they can track the movements of these terrifying storms. A storm's huge size, spinning motion, spiral shape, bands of thick rain-bearing clouds, and tiny circular eye are all clearly visible from space.

Rotation of hurricane

Direction of hurricane

TORNADO FACT FILE

Wind speed	65–300 mph
Speed across the ground	Usually about 30 mph, but up to 70 mph
Lifetime	A few seconds to more than an hour
Biggest tornado	2.6 miles wide at its base, near El Reno, Oklahoma, on May 31, 2013
Deadliest tornado	Bangladesh (1989), killed 1,300 people
Deadliest U.S. tornado	Tri-State Tornado (1925), killed 695 people in Missouri, Illinois, and Indiana
Where tornadoes are found	Every continent except Antarctica
U.S. state with the most tornadoes	Texas (125 a year on average)

Wedge tornadoes

Most tornadoes are tall and thin, but a few are at least as wide as they are tall. Although these tornadoes are enormous, size doesn't always show how intense or damaging a tornado is. Some wedge tornadoes can be very damaging indeed, but they are not always so violent.

TWISTERS

One of the strangest, scariest, and most destructive things that can be seen in the sky is a tornado. They're also called twisters. A tornado is a column of air spinning at high speed as it moves across the ground. The column is often the shape of a funnel: wide at the top and narrow at the bottom. Tornadoes form in places where hot, moist air meets cool, dry air. Many of them are produced by giant rotating thunderclouds called supercells. The most extreme tornadoes whip up winds fast enough to tear trees out of the ground and smash houses to pieces.

Devastation

The fastest and most damaging winds blow around the narrow base of a tornado. As the tornado travels across the ground, it leaves a trail of devastation behind. Pieces of wood, street signs, and even objects as heavy as cars are picked up by the tornado and turned into missiles. The tornado hurls them through the air, causing even more damage.

Dust devils

A dust devil is a tornado's little brother. It forms when hot air rises very quickly and begins to rotate, sucking in more air and loose dirt.

Spotting tornadoes

Tornadoes are sometimes spotted reaching down to the ground below the most severe thunderclouds. The base of the tornado, where it touches the ground, is often surrounded by a cloud of dirt and debris stirred up by the fast-spinning wind.

Falling air

Rising air

Direction of tornado

Direction of rotation

Inside a twister

A tornado sucks air along the ground toward it. As the air spirals in, it speeds up. Inside the tornado, the air spirals upward and spills out at the top. At the same time, more air is sucked down into the tornado from above.

CANADA

Cold, dry wind from the north

Tornado Alley

UNITED STATES

Jet stream

Warm, moist air from the Gulf of Mexico

Hot, dry wind from the desert

Gulf of Mexico

MEXICO

Tornado alley

Tornadoes occur in every state of the United States, but they are most common in a central region called Tornado Alley. It's where warm, moist air from the south meets cold, dry air from the north and hot, dry air from the west. These are perfect conditions for creating supercell thunderstorms, which can produce tornadoes.

Charting strength

A tornado's strength is measured on a scale called the Enhanced Fujita Scale. It goes from EF-0, the weakest, to EF-5, the strongest. An EF-0 tornado might break some tree branches, but an EF-5 tornado is powerful enough to pick up a house.

Enhanced Fujita (EF) Scale

Scale	Category	Wind speed	Possible damage
EF-0	Weak	65–85 mph	Light: tree branches broken, signs damaged
EF-1	Weak	86–110 mph	Moderate: trees snapped, mobile homes pushed off foundations or overturned, windows broken
EF-2	Strong	111–135 mph	Significant: large trees snapped or uprooted, weak structures destroyed
EF-3	Strong	136–165 mph	Severe: some roofs torn off framed houses, trees leveled
EF-4	Violent	166–200 mph	Devastating: roofs and some walls torn off well-constructed houses, cars thrown or overturned
EF-5	Violent	More than 200 mph	Incredible: houses may be lifted off foundation, structures the size of cars can be thrown over 300 feet, steel-reinforced buildings highly damaged

Chasing storms

Some people like to study the most extreme weather up close. They hunt for thunderstorms and tornadoes. They often travel in armored vehicles to protect themselves from the wind and debris that is blown around.

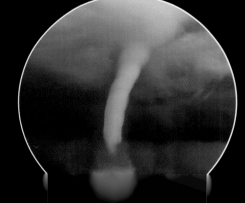

Waterspouts

Waterspouts look like tornadoes on water. Some of them are indeed tornadoes. Others are different, forming in light winds. Waterspouts are usually weaker than tornadoes, but they can still damage boats, so sailors steer clear of them.

Highest air temperature	134°F at Furnace Creek, Death Valley, California, on July 10, 1913
Highest surface temperature	159.3°F in the Lut Desert, Iran, in 2005
Fastest rise in temperature	49°F in two minutes in Spearfish, South Dakota, on January 22, 1943
Hottest continent	Africa
Hottest U.S. states	Florida, Hawaii, Louisiana, and Texas
Warmest ocean	Indian Ocean

Desert animals

Hot deserts are very difficult places to live in. Desert animals are specially adapted to the heat and shortage of water. They try to stay out of the sun as much as possible during the day, and they don't waste a single drop of water.

EXTREME HEAT

The hottest parts of our planet are the dry, sun-drenched deserts near the equator. Under clear skies, the land soaks up energy from the sun and the temperature soars. Places like this are very difficult to live in. The temperature is so high in the hottest deserts that someone out in the open without any protection from the heat would die quickly. Places where the air is humid (moist) as well as very hot are the most uncomfortable, because the human body can't sweat to lose heat in these conditions. One answer is to live underground or in caves.

Caribbean

Not all of the world's hottest places are dry deserts. The lush green islands of the Caribbean lie close to the equator. With the sun almost overhead, they are very hot all year round.

Death Valley

The hottest place in North America is the scarily named Death Valley. It's a long, narrow, and deep desert valley in the eastern part of California. The highest air temperature ever recorded in nature on earth was measured in a part of Death Valley called Furnace Creek.

Desert hot spots

The Lut Desert in Iran is sometimes called the hottest place on earth. There are no weather stations there, but its temperature was measured by a spacecraft called *Aqua*. It recorded a ground temperature of 159.3°F.

Hot interior

Uluru, also known as Ayers Rock, is a giant mound of rock that rises out of the vast, hot desert that forms the interior of Australia. At the nearby town of Alice Springs, a temperature of 120.6°F was recorded on January 3, 2006.

The vast Sahara

The Sahara in North Africa is the world's biggest hot desert. It is almost as big as the United States and reaches temperatures of more than 176°F in places.

Living underground

Coober Pedy, a town in South Australia, is known for two things. It is the center of Australia's opal mining industry. It is also famous for underground homes carved out of the rock. While the temperature in homes on the surface often reaches 104°F, the rock homes are cooler.

Afar Depression

The Afar Depression is a low-lying part of Ethiopia in the Horn of Africa. The landscape is very hot, dry, and inhospitable. Three of the giant plates of rock that form the earth's crust meet there, so earthquakes are common.

Area of land covered by forest	About 10 billion acres worldwide
Percentage of forests consumed by fire every year	1%, or about 100 million acres
Biggest ever forest fire	The Miramichi Fire in New Brunswick, Canada, in 1825. It covered an area of 3 million acres.
Deadliest U.S. forest fire	The Peshtigo Fire in 1871. Up to 2,500 people were killed.
Temperature of a forest fire	1,470–2,190°F
Highest fire lookout post	Dave Evans Bicentennial Tree in Warren National Park, southwestern Australia, 223 feet
Causes of forest fires	80–90% started by people, the rest by lightning

Regrowth

After a brush fire, the ground often looks lifeless, but seeds and roots buried in the dirt may be undamaged. New plants start growing again within days or weeks, and the area quickly recovers.

HEAT WAVES AND WILDFIRES

People can get used to living in places that are hot all the time, but a rise in temperature somewhere that isn't usually very hot—a heat wave—can be uncomfortable or even dangerous. A heat wave can last for days or weeks. In a severe heat wave there can be tens of thousands more deaths than normal. Heat waves can also make travel more difficult by melting roads and buckling railway lines. When thousands or even millions of people turn on air conditioners and fans to try to keep cool, the steep rise in demand for electricity can trigger power cuts.

High pressure "cap"

What causes a heat wave

Heat waves happen when a bubble of high-pressure hot air settles over the land and stays there. It prevents hot air on the ground from rising and blowing away as it would usually do. If the air can't rise, it can't form rain clouds either. A heat wave lasts until nearby weather systems move the bubble of hot air away.

Melting tarmac, New Delhi

In May 2015, roads in the Indian capital of New Delhi started melting because the country was in the grip of a heat wave. Temperatures were the highest in 20 years. On May 21, New Delhi reached 108.7°F. It was even hotter elsewhere. More than 2,500 people died. The temperature finally fell when the monsoon rains arrived on June 3.

Smoke jumpers

Fires in the middle of large, thick forests are sometimes impossible for firefighters to reach by land. One way to deal with them is to drop water on them from aircraft. Another way is to use firefighters called smoke jumpers. They parachute into forest clearings to deal with the fires.

Watching for fires

Forests in some places, especially in the United States, are monitored by lookouts at the top of towers. The lookouts watch for smoke and lightning strikes. Many of the lookout towers have now been replaced by automatic sensors and aircraft patrols.

Wildfires

Heat waves dry out vegetation and it soon becomes a fire hazard. Then all it takes is a spark, lightning, or a careless camper lighting a fire to start a raging blaze that can be very hard to stop. Brush fires can burn for days or even weeks. They can destroy homes, forests, and crops.

Coldest place on earth	Vostok Station, Antarctica. On July 21, 1983, the temperature reached -128.56°F.
Coldest city on earth	Yakutsk, Russia
Coldest inhabited places	Oymyakon and Verkhoyansk, Russia
Coldest place in U.S.	Prospect Creek, Alaska; on January 23, 1971, the temperature reached -80°F.
Coldest possible temperature	Absolute zero (-459.67°F)
Greatest snowfall in one storm	189 inches at the Mount Shasta Ski Bowl in February 1959
Fastest temperature drop	49°F in 15 minutes in Rapid City, South Dakota, on January 10, 1911

Blizzards

A blizzard is heavy snow blown by a strong wind. The windblown snow is difficult to walk through, and it's also hard for drivers to see the roads. The snow piles up in deep drifts.

EXTREME COLD

Unusually cold weather can be caused by shifts in wind patterns that bring blasts of icy air far farther south than normal. When the temperature plunges below freezing in places that aren't used to such cold weather, life becomes more difficult. People without enough warm clothing or heating at home risk a life-threatening condition called hypothermia. Young children and elderly people are especially at risk. Rivers and canals freeze. The ground is as hard as stone. Crops can be wiped out. Roads may be covered with slippery snow and ice, bringing traffic to a standstill. Ports and airports struggle to stay open. Normal life can become impossible.

A frozen Hudson River

The Hudson River in New York City rarely freezes, but it froze at the beginning of 2014 and again at the beginning of 2015. The reason for such unusually low temperatures was a "cold wave," a shift in the normal weather patterns that sent freezing air flooding down over eastern North America. Hundreds of temperature and snowfall records—some of which had stood for a century or more—were smashed in several states.

Deicing planes

A plane's ability to fly depends on the special shape of its wings. If ice forms on the wings, it spoils this special shape. Ice could also be sucked into the engines and damage them, so planes are often deiced before takeoff in freezing weather.

Ice storm

An extreme weather event called an ice storm can transform buildings into fairy tale ice palaces. Rain falling onto frozen surfaces quickly freezes and coats the surface with a glaze of ice. The weight of the ice can bring down tree branches and power lines.

Avalanche

If snow builds up on sloping ground, there is a danger that it may suddenly break free and slide down in a deadly collapse called an avalanche. The biggest and fastest avalanches can send millions of tons of snow tumbling down the side of a mountain at more than 185 mph. Ski slopes are kept safe by starting small avalanches deliberately so that dangerously deep snow cannot build up and cause a bigger and more destructive avalanche.

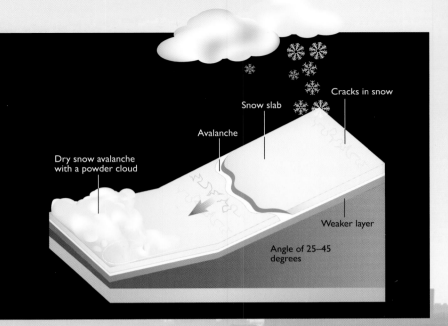

Cracks in snow

Snow slab

Avalanche

Dry snow avalanche with a powder cloud

Weaker layer

Angle of 25–45 degrees

Frozen falls

Climbers rarely get the chance to climb a waterfall, but extreme cold has the power to turn a waterfall into an icy climbing wall. Even the mighty Niagara Falls can be brought to a frozen standstill.

Lowest Arctic temperature	-90°F
Lowest Antarctic temperature	-128.56°F
Thickness of Arctic ice	10–13 feet
Thickness of Antarctic ice	Up to 13,000 feet
Windiest continent	Antarctica
Coldest continent	Antarctica
First submarine to cross the Arctic Ocean under the ice	USS Nautilus in 1958
First person to cross the ice to the North Pole	Ralph Plaisted (1968)
First person to cross the ice to the South Pole	Roald Amundsen (1911)

Wildlife

The animals that live near the poles find their food in the sea, or hunt each other. The top predator in the Arctic is the polar bear. The best-known Antarctic creature is the penguin.

POLAR WEATHER

The weather at the earth's poles is so bitterly cold that explorers and scientists are the only people who venture there. The temperature at the poles almost never rises above freezing point, so the surface is permanently covered with ice. Most of the Arctic ice is only about 10–13 feet thick. The Antarctic ice is much thicker, up to 13,000 feet in places. The chilling effect of the huge expanse of polar ice produces powerful winds and ocean currents that help move air and water around the whole planet.

The poles

Earth's polar regions look alike, but they are different. They are almost mirror images of each other. The Arctic is an ice-covered ocean surrounded by land. The Antarctic is ice-covered land surrounded by an ocean.

Arctic

The Arctic consists of the Arctic Ocean and parts of the countries around it. The Arctic Ocean, the smallest of the world's oceans, is covered by a sheet of ice that grows and shrinks each year.

Antarctica

Antarctica is a continent about twice the size of Australia. It contains nearly all of the ice on Earth. If all of it were to melt, the sea level all over the world would rise at least 200 feet.

The polar landscape

At the North and South Poles, there is ice as far as you can see in all directions. At the South Pole there are rock outcrops called nunataks. These are the tops of mountains buried under the ice. As there is no land at the North Pole, there are no such rocky outcrops there.

Research stations

There are several research stations in Antarctica where scientists work, studying the continent. A serious problem faced by the stations is that their buildings are buried by the constant blizzards and snowfall. It takes about ten years to bury a building in Antarctica.

Amundsen-Scott South Pole Station

A new South Pole research station has been designed to solve the problems the old stations faced. The snow will not bury this one. The Amundsen-Scott South Pole Station's odd shape keeps snow from piling up under and around it. If the snow does begin to bury it, the whole building can be jacked up higher.

South Pole

Lake Vostok

Under the ice

A liquid water lake, Lake Vostok, lies underneath 13,000 feet of ice in Antarctica. It has been cut off from the rest of the planet for millions of years. Scientists are drilling down into it to search for new forms of life. The ice itself holds a record of Earth's climate stretching back thousands of years.

Icebergs

When glaciers reach the sea, they break up and the ice floats away as icebergs. The ice, made of frozen fresh water, floats in the denser seawater. Icebergs are made in both the Arctic and Antarctic. The part of an iceberg that stands above the water is only about one-eighth of the whole iceberg. The rest lies below the surface. As an iceberg melts, it can become top-heavy and suddenly roll over. This can create a huge wave, so boats stay a safe distance away.

Deadliest flood	China (1931); up to 4 million people died and 80 million were left homeless.
Worst U.S. flood	The Great Mississippi Flood of 1927 covered an area of 27,000 square miles.
Depth of moving water that will knock a person over	6 inches
Depth of moving water that will float a car away	2 feet
Potential depth of flash floods	20 feet

Hidden dangers

Wading through floodwater can be very risky. Floods can wash dangerous wild creatures into towns and villages. Snakes and even crocodiles can lurk unseen beneath the muddy water.

FLOODS

Floods can turn vast areas of dry land into lakes. They can destroy homes, bring transportation to a halt, cut power supplies, pollute water, and turn farmland into mud. Fast-moving floodwater has enormous power. It can wash buildings and cars away altogether. The most serious flooding is caused by heavy rainfall or melting snow. It's worse if the ground is already frozen or waterlogged, or rivers are already high when the floodwater arrives. High tides and storm surges can make flooding even worse. The water level may rise slowly or the flood can arrive suddenly as a flash flood.

A thousand-year flood

In May 2010, up to 20 inches of rain fell on parts of Tennessee in only two days. Rivers overflowed and there was widespread flooding. It was such an extreme event that Tennessee might expect it to happen only once every 1,000 years.

Flash flood

Flash floods develop so quickly that they soon overwhelm the ability of the land and drains to take the water away. They can turn roads and valleys into raging torrents.

The Red River flood

Amphibious (floating) excavators break up an ice jam on the Red River in Manitoba, Canada. The river flooded in March 2009 because a huge volume of water from heavy rain and melting snow could not escape. It was held back by ice jams that blocked the river. Once these were cleared, the water level began to fall.

Boscastle

On August 16, 2004, the coastal village of Boscastle, England, suffered one of the worst flash floods ever experienced in that country. Six buildings and 75 cars were washed into the sea, and dozens more buildings were destroyed. A fleet of seven helicopters rescued 150 people.

Monsoon

The monsoon winds that blow inland from the Indian Ocean are loaded with moisture. As the air rises over the hot land, it cools down and forms rain. The torrential downpours it produces can cause severe flooding.

Driest place on earth	Dry Valleys, Antarctica—no rain for 2 million years
Driest place on earth not in the polar regions	Atacama Desert, Chile—average rainfall 0.6 inch per year
Longest drought in history	400 years—Atacama Desert, Chile, from 1571 to 1971
Deadliest drought	Droughts and floods in China from 1958 to 1961 led to a famine that killed up to 43 million people.
Worst U.S. drought	The Dust Bowl in the 1930s affected 100 million acres.

Crop damage

During a drought, farm crops cannot take up enough water from the soil. The roots begin to die and the plants wilt. Pests and diseases attack the weakened plants and the crop fails.

DROUGHTS

A drought is an unusually dry period of weather when there is low rainfall, or none at all. It can last from a few days to many years. Water is essential for all life on earth, so droughts can be catastrophic for people, animals, and crops. As the land dries out, there is also a greater risk of wildfires. Crop failures caused by drought can lead to famine in some places, too.

Rocket fired from aircraft

Rain

Rockets fired from land

Cloud seeding

It is possible to produce rain by releasing chemicals into clouds. Moisture collects on the chemical particles and forms raindrops, which then fall onto crops. Cloud seeding is used by several countries, including the United States and China.

California drought

By 2014, after several years of severe drought, reservoirs in California held a fraction of their normal water volumes. The water level in one of them, Lake Shasta, had fallen by 200 feet. The lake held less than a third of the water it normally contains, its lowest level since the 1970s.

Amazon drought

Part of the Amazon rain forest, which is twice the size of California, has been affected by a drought that began in 2005. The forest started to recover as rainfall returned to normal, but then it was struck by an even worse drought in 2010.

Desalination

One way to deal with water shortages is to make fresh water from seawater. This is called desalination. If seawater is heated, it evaporates, leaving the salt behind. Then the vapor is cooled to change it back to water. Another method pushes the water through a membrane that traps the salt.

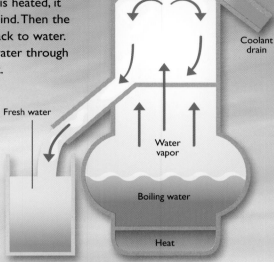

Cooling water

Condensing dome

Coolant drain

Fresh water

Water vapor

Boiling water

Heat

Dust Bowl

In the 1930s, a drought that lasted for most of the decade turned the Great Plains of the United States to dust. Crops failed and animals died. More than two million people had to leave the area to look for work elsewhere. This natural disaster is known as the Dust Bowl.

Occurrence of El Niño	Every 3–7 years
Arrival date	December
Typical weather effects of El Niño on the United States	Drier along eastern seaboard, December–May Wetter southern states, September–February Warmer northwest, January–May Cooler southern states, December–April
Typical weather effects of La Niña on the United States	Drier southern states, December–February Warmer southern states, October–April Warmer in the northeast, July–October Cooler in the northwest, February–November

Flooding

The rainfall in some parts of the world increases so much during El Niño and La Niña years that flooding is far more likely. Knowing this helps the countries at most risk to prepare for the worst.

EL NIÑO AND LA NIÑA

The oceans have a powerful effect on the weather. The water cools or warms the air above it. Changes in the air temperature affect wind and rainfall over a wide area. Even places that are far inland, a long way from any coast, are affected by the oceans. The Pacific Ocean is so big that it can alter the weather all over the world. Normally, winds blow from east to west across the Pacific, moving warm water toward the west, but events called El Niño and La Niña change the Pacific weather patterns every few years. These changes have been linked to changes in the weather of other countries.

Tropical storm

In an El Niño year, there is increased rainfall and flooding in Peru, and droughts in Indonesia, India, and parts of Brazil. In a La Niña year, the wet weather shifts to the other side of the Pacific Ocean, causing increased rainfall in Southeast Asia.

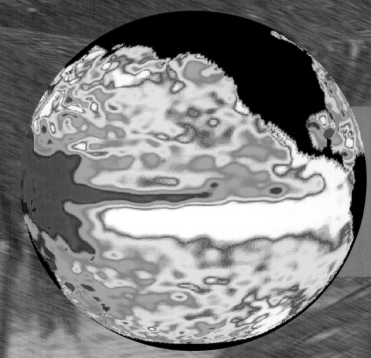

How El Niño happens

In an El Niño year, the Pacific winds weaken. Warm water that is usually blown westward stays in the east. Satellites in space can detect the change in temperature. The air above the warmer water is heated, rises, and produces more rain across the Americas.

How La Niña happens

In La Niña years, the Pacific winds blow westward more strongly than normal. They blow more warm water to the western side of the ocean. It warms the moist air above it, which rises and forms rain clouds, increasing rainfall in Asia.

A normal year

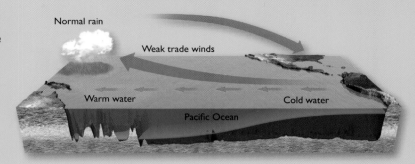

Normal rain

Weak trade winds

Warm water

Cold water

Pacific Ocean

A La Niña year

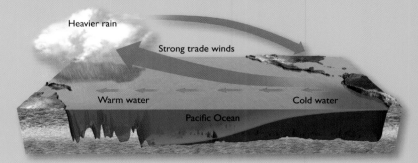

Heavier rain

Strong trade winds

Warm water

Cold water

Pacific Ocean

Mosquitoes

The warmer, wetter weather in parts of South America during El Niño years enables mosquitoes to breed in greater numbers. They include mosquitoes that carry diseases such as malaria and dengue fever.

Peru fishing

Fishermen in Peru dread the arrival of El Niño, because the fish they depend on disappear. The fish either die out or move elsewhere because of changes in the ocean currents and water temperature.

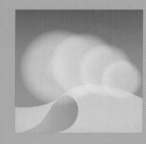

How high can sand or dust be blown by the wind?	20,000 feet
Worst sandstorm	Black Sunday occurred on April 14, 1935, during the American Dust Bowl and displaced more than 300,000 tons of soil.
Protection against a sandstorm	Desert people wear long robes and veils. Camels can close their nostrils to keep the sand out. They also use a third eyelid to brush away sand.
Number of people killed by air pollution every year	3 million worldwide
Country with the most polluted cities in the world	13 of the world's 20 most polluted cities are in India, including the world's most polluted: Delhi.

Air pollution

The air quality in some cities is sometimes so poor that people wear face masks when they go outside. The masks help to filter out the pollution and reduce the risk of breathing problems and illness.

SANDSTORMS AND SMOG

Fresh air is crystal clear and odorless, but sandstorms and smog can turn it into a choking soup. Sand and dust are so light that the wind can pick them up and blow them around. Smog is a mixture of smoke and fog. Smoke usually rises and blows away because it's hotter and lighter than the surrounding air, but if it mixes with cold fog, it clings to the ground. Some cities suffer from a different type of smog, a chemical smog made from the smoke and gases pumped out by vehicle engines and factories.

Sand in the rain

Desert sand can be blown a long way before it falls to the ground. These motorcycles in Spain are covered with sand blown more than 2,000 miles from Africa. Sand from Africa can even cross the Atlantic Ocean and land in North America.

L.A. smog

Los Angeles suffers from worse air pollution and smog than most U.S. cities. It's caused by exhaust gases and sooty particles produced by heavy traffic, and made worse by the shape of the ground. L.A. sits in a bowl-shaped basin that traps the smog so that it builds up instead of blowing away.

Dusty sunset

Sand in the air can intensify the red color of the sky at sunset. The sand acts like countless mirrors reflecting sunlight. As the sunlight travels toward us, air molecules scatter out the blue part of the light, turning it red.

Dust Bowl

The drought that struck the United States in the 1930s is known as the Dust Bowl because the dust-dry soil was so light that it simply blew away. Vast dust storms turned day to night.

Dust Bowl states

Severe dust storm damage

Other areas with dust storm damage

Shanghai smog

Shanghai, China, disappears under clouds of smog. Poor air quality is a problem in many other Chinese cities too. The main cause is the large amount of coal that is burned to make electricity.

Sandstorm in Jordan

When strong winds whip up sandstorms in Jordan's eastern desert, visibility can be so poor that major highways have to be closed. These hot, dry, dusty winds, known as *khamsin* in the Middle East, return every year between April and June.

EARTHQUAKE FACT FILE

Number of earthquakes worldwide every year	500,000
Number of earthquakes that can be felt each year	100,000
Number of earthquakes that cause damage each year	100
Biggest recorded earthquake	A magnitude 9.5 earthquake in Chile on May 22, 1960
Biggest earthquake in the United States	A magnitude 9.2 earthquake on Prince William Sound, Alaska, on March 28, 1964
Most earthquake-prone U.S. state	Alaska: about 24,000 a year
Deadliest earthquake	Central China in 1556, killing 830,000 people
Deadliest earthquake in the last 100 years	Tangshan, China, in 1976, killing 250,000 people
Earliest recorded earthquake	Shandong Province, China, in 1831 BC

Nepal quake

On April 25, 2015, Nepal suffered a severe earthquake, the worst natural disaster in the small Himalayan country for 80 years. More than 9,000 people were killed and 23,000 were injured.

EARTHQUAKES

The ground seems safe, solid, and unmoving. Usually it is, but sometimes it can suddenly start shaking. The shaking is an earthquake. It can be violent enough to bring buildings crashing down. Small earthquakes called foreshocks warn that something bigger may be on the way. Then the main shock, the strongest earthquake, is followed by a series of aftershocks.

Northridge earthquake

Los Angeles experienced a strong earthquake in 1994. It was named after a part of the city called Northridge. Roads and buildings were badly damaged. Building regulations were changed after the earthquake to make buildings more able to withstand future quakes.

Rescue teams

After a powerful earthquake, it is vital to find survivors trapped in collapsed buildings quickly. Search-and-rescue teams use dogs because they can sniff out people hidden in the wreckage.

San Andreas fault

Two parts of the earth's crust meet on the west coast of the United States. The fault between the two plates is called the San Andreas fault. It runs through the state of California, where it has caused a number of serious earthquakes.

Moving plates

An earthquake happens when two of the vast plates of rock (tectonic plates) that form the earth's crust suddenly slip past each other. The place where they meet is called a fault. The plates may have been trying to move for years but were locked together until they finally broke free and shifted.

Chile earthquake

The most powerful earthquake ever recorded struck Chile on May 22, 1960. It's called the Valvidia earthquake. The ground shook for 10 minutes. Thousands of buildings collapsed and numerous landslides were triggered. Up to 6,000 people died.

Christchurch

New Zealand stands on the fault between the Australian plate and the Pacific plate. Movements of these plates cause earthquakes. On February 22, 2011, New Zealand suffered a damaging earthquake centered on the city of Christchurch.

TSUNAMI FACT FILE

Speed of a tsunami across the ocean	Up to 500 mph
Speed of a tsunami when it makes landfall	20–30 mph
Biggest tsunami in recorded history	Lituya Bay, Alaska, in 1958. The waves were 1,700 feet high.
Deadliest tsunami	A tsunami in the Indian Ocean in 2004 killed more than 200,000 people in 14 countries.
U.S. state at greatest tsunami risk	Hawaii

Power station disaster

The Fukushima Daiichi nuclear power station in Japan was struck by a 50-foot-high tsunami on March 11, 2011. The station was so badly damaged that more than 100,000 people were evacuated from the area because of the danger from radiation.

TSUNAMIS

One of the most terrifying and destructive natural disasters is a tsunami. It's a series of ocean waves that can be as high as 100 feet or more. Tsunamis can be caused by landslides and volcanoes, but the worst tsunamis are caused by underwater earthquakes. When these huge walls of water reach land, they cause widespread destruction. They can sweep away whole towns. They travel so fast that they can cross an ocean in a day. Most tsunamis happen in the Pacific Ocean, because its Ring of Fire produces so many earthquakes and volcanic eruptions.

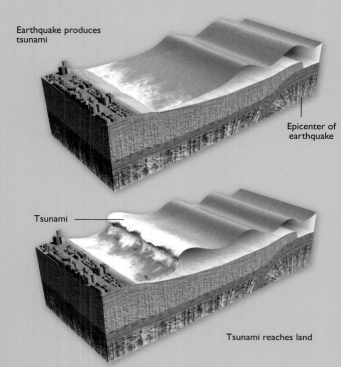

Earthquake produces tsunami

Epicenter of earthquake

Tsunami

Tsunami reaches land

How tsunamis start

When one part of the earth's crust slides under another part, the edge of the top part is dragged downward. It slowly bends like a giant spring. Eventually, it snaps free and bounces upward, lifting the sea above it. The raised pile of water flows away in all directions as a series of waves, a tsunami. As the waves reach shallow water near land, the front of each wave slows down and the water piles up higher and higher.

Tsunami waves

Huge waves overtop a seawall and swallow a town at the mouth of the Hei River as a tsunami arrives on the coast of Japan in 2011. Vehicles are swept away like toys, wooden buildings are smashed to pieces, and farmland near the coast is flooded.

Lisbon

Europe is not known for disastrous tsunamis, but they have happened in the past. One of the deadliest struck Lisbon, Portugal, on November 1, 1755. Up to 60,000 people were killed by a severe earthquake that was followed by 20-foot-high waves.

High and dry

A tsunami leaves a clear record of how serious it was. The height the waves reached can be seen from the debris they carried with them and left behind. Boats are often carried inland and left high and dry. Some of them even end up sitting on top of buildings.

Devastation

On March 11, 2011, Japan was struck by the most powerful earthquake ever to hit the country. It produced a tsunami up to 133 feet high in places that swept inland. Coastal towns were devastated. More than 15,000 people died and 6,000 were injured.

World's worst landslide	Gansu, China, on December 16, 1920. More than 180,000 people were killed.
Biggest landslide in recorded history	Eruption of Mount St. Helens in Washington in 1980. Enough rock to fill 250 million trucks slid 14 miles.
States reporting the most damage from sinkholes	Florida, Texas, Alabama, Missouri, Kentucky, Tennessee, and Pennsylvania
Sinkhole size	From a few feet across to hundreds of acres, and from a few inches to 100 feet deep
Area of United States susceptible to sinkholes	20 percent
Parts of United States prone to landslides	Western coast ranges Cascades volcanic region Central and northern Rocky Mountains Appalachian region Mississippi River and tributaries

Making cliffs secure

Cliffs in danger of collapsing can be saved by covering them with steel mesh held in place by long bolts driven into the rock. The mesh acts as a strong safety net, holding the rock together.

SHIFTING GROUND

Ground that seems solid and safe can sometimes give way without warning. The edge of a cliff may collapse. A hillside may suddenly start sliding, shedding rock and earth onto the ground below. Heavy rain can turn solid ground into a fast-moving river of mud. Even more worrying, deep holes big enough to swallow a house can suddenly open up in the ground. Some of these holes, called sinkholes, are caused when the rock under the surface simply dissolves away. Others happen when the ground is weakened by old mine tunnels or water from leaking pipes.

Sliding cliffs

The pounding of waves at the bottom of cliffs washes out rock and earth. Eventually, there is nothing to support the weight of the ground above and the cliff collapses into the sea.

Landslide

Roads cut through hillsides risk being blocked by landslides. The landslides are often caused by rain. Rain soaking into the ground works like oil in an engine. It lets parts of the ground slide over each other more easily.

Disappearing

Houses built on land with unknown sinkholes or mine shafts hidden below are in danger of sinking into the ground. The first sign of trouble might be cracks appearing in walls and floors as the ground begins to move.

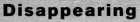

Cenotes

The Yucatán Peninsula in Mexico is peppered with thousands of water-filled holes. They're known as cenotes. These are sinkholes caused by rainwater draining down through the ground and dissolving limestone rock below the surface. Big caverns slowly open up, covered by a thin roof of rock and earth. Eventually the roof falls in, forming the cenote.

Holes in roads

Sinkholes sometimes appear in the middle of roads. The weight of new roads and buildings can make the roof of a sinkhole below them collapse. The hole might have formed because water from a leaking water pipe or a broken drain washed soil away.

Mudslide

If sloping ground becomes waterlogged, it can become so loose and slippery that a whole hillside breaks away and turns into a muddy, watery avalanche. Mudslides are very dangerous because they move so fast. A large mudslide can bury a building or even a whole village in just a few minutes.

Number of active volcanoes	About 1,500
Number of active volcanoes in the United States	65
The deadliest volcano	Mount Tambora in Indonesia (1815). It killed about 92,000 people.
Biggest active volcano on land	Mount Mauna Loa in Hawaii
Biggest active volcano in Europe	Mount Etna, Sicily
Most active volcano on earth	Mount Yasur, Vanuatu—it has been erupting for more than 800 years.
Last supervolcano eruption on earth	Mount Toba, Indonesia, 74,000 years ago
Southernmost active volcano	Mount Erebus, Antarctica
Famous volcanic eruptions	Vesuvius (79) Krakatoa (1883) Novarupta (1912) Mount St. Helens (1980) Mount Pinatubo (1991)

Pompeii

The Italian town of Pompeii is famous for the preserved remains of some of its people. They died when a nearby volcano, Mount Vesuvius, erupted in 79, burying the whole town in ash.

VOLCANOES AND ASH CLOUDS

An erupting volcano is an awesome sight and also extremely dangerous. Volcanoes are openings in the earth's crust that let hot liquid rock from deep underground pour out onto the surface. Some eruptions are explosive. They blast fiery fountains of lava (melted rock) and thick clouds of choking ash high in the air. The biggest volcanic eruptions send so much ash into the atmosphere that they can dim the sun and change the weather all over the world. Amazingly, about 500 million people live near active volcanoes.

Acid rain

Erupting volcanoes give out enormous amounts of gas. The gas reacts with moisture in the air and forms droplets of acid. This may fall to the ground as acid rain. The acid is strong enough to eat into metal. It can also damage plants or even kill them.

How a volcano forms

Volcanoes often form in places called subduction zones. These are places where one of the earth's crust plates slides under another plate. As the plates grind against each other, the temperature climbs until the rock melts. It rises to the surface and bursts out as a volcano. Most earthquakes and volcanic eruptions happen around the edge of the massive Pacific plate, the biggest of the plates of rock that form the earth's surface. There are so many volcanoes here that it is called the Ring of Fire.

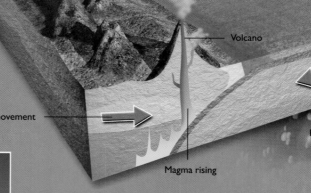

Volcano

Plate movement

Plate movement

Magma rising

Ash cloud

The vast clouds of ash that pour out of erupting volcanoes are made of tiny jagged pieces of rock and glass. They range in size from fine powder to pieces the size of a grain of sand. They're made when gas bubbles in lava burst and blow the lava apart.

Lava fountains

Kilauea on the island of Hawaii is one of the world's most active volcanoes. It has been erupting nonstop since 1983. It's famous for spectacular lava fountains that send red-hot lava spraying and splashing out of the mountaintop.

Icelandic blast

When a volcano called Eyjafjallajökull on Iceland erupted in April 2010, it produced an enormous cloud of ash. Wind spread the ash cloud across Europe. Worries about the damage it might do to aircraft engines led to the biggest air travel shutdown since World War II.

Mount St. Helens

Mount St. Helens (above), a volcano in Washington, blew its top in 1980 with the power of 1,600 atomic bombs. When the air cleared, it looked very different (below). The top 1,300 feet of the mountain had disappeared.

Number of lakes on earth	117 million
Number of lakes at risk of limnic eruptions	3
Number of limnic eruptions in recorded history	2
Number of people killed by limnic eruptions in the past 100 years	1,737
Rise in water level due to an extreme seiche	6–30 feet

Lake Kivu

Scientists think gas erupts from Lake Kivu in central Africa every 1,000 years or so, but no one knows exactly when the next eruption will happen. When it does, two million people living around the lake could be in danger.

LAKE HAZARDS

Lakes look like calm bodies of water, but some lakes have hidden dangers. A small number of lakes can produce a deadly natural disaster called a limnic eruption. If a lake has a lot of gas dissolved in its water and then a landslide or earthquake stirs it up, the effect is like opening a bottle of soda. Gas suddenly bubbles out. A lake can produce enough gas to kill people and animals nearby. Another strange event seen in lakes, harbors, or bays is called a seiche. It can make the water level at the edge of a lake rise suddenly. Extreme seiches can produce dangerous flooding.

Making lakes safe

Lakes in danger of producing limnic eruptions can be made safe by removing gas from them. It's done by sinking a pipe down to the bottom of the lake. When the deep, gas-filled water floods into the pipe, the gas rushes to the surface, pushing out a fountain of water.

Disaster

Lake Nyos in Cameroon, central Africa, is normally a calm and quiet lake, but that changed without warning on the night of August 21, 1986. A huge cloud of carbon dioxide gas bubbled out of the lake. Carbon dioxide is heavier than air, so it flowed downhill into nearby valleys, where it killed 1,700 people and hundreds of animals.

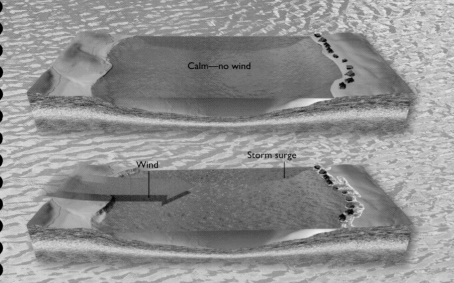

Calm—no wind

Wind

Storm surge

Great Lakes

Seiches occur on North America's Great Lakes. Most of them are very small, but there have been times when a seiche has sent waves up to 20 feet high crashing onto the shore.

How seiches happen

When wind keeps blowing in the same direction, it can push water from one side of a lake or bay to the other. The water piles up at one side. Then if the wind drops or changes direction, the water flows back again and carries on sloshing back and forth.

Shaky lakes

Lake Tahoe in the United States has suffered from seiches in the past, but they were not caused by wind. Instead, they were caused by earthquakes. An earthquake causes a seiche by shaking a lake. It can also set off landslides on the shore that launch waves across the lake and trigger a seiche.

Venice

Venice stands at the northern end of the long, narrow Adriatic Sea. Parts of Venice are often flooded by high tides, but the flooding is sometimes made worse by a seiche that raises the sea level at Venice every 22 hours. It happens when wind pushes water north toward Venice.

Total number of satellites launched	6,600
Number of satellites still in orbit in 2015	3,600
Number of satellites still working in 2015	About 1,000
Number of weather satellites launched	Approximately 86
Number of weather satellites still working in 2015	Approximately 30
Altitude reached by a weather balloon	About 25 miles
Speed of a weather forecasting supercomputer	16,000 trillion calculations per second
Number of observations used for weather forecasting	500,000 a day

Weather buoy

There are hundreds of floating weather buoys in the oceans. They send their weather data to satellites, which relay them to weather forecasters.

FORECAST AND RESEARCH

If people can be warned when a natural disaster or extreme weather is about to happen, lives can be saved. Measuring tiny movements in the ground gives clues to when an earthquake might happen or a volcano might erupt. Earth's atmosphere is watched and measured in great detail too. A huge amount of information is collected every day. Superfast computers use this information to determine how the weather will change in the near future. These forecasts can warn people if a dangerous storm is coming their way or if flooding is expected.

Space watch

Dozens of weather satellites point their cameras and scientific instruments at Earth. They track the clouds moving around the world. They watch hurricanes forming. They can also see smoke from large forest fires and ash pouring out of erupting volcanoes.

Using radio

Rainclouds can be found and tracked by radio. Radio waves are sent out into the sky. Some of them bounce back from raindrops. The time the radio waves take to bounce back and the direction they come from show where the rainclouds are. Using radio in this way is called radar.

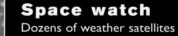

Making lightning

Scientists who study lightning would like it to strike the same spot again and again. They do it by launching small rockets into thunderclouds. Lightning travels down a wire trailing from the rocket or a stream of gas left behind by the rocket. The wire or gas leads the lightning down to the same spot over and over again.

Storm watch

Storm chasers specialize in gathering information about the most severe storms and tornadoes. They carry computers, cameras, and scientific instruments to record weather data. They measure the wind speed and direction, temperature, humidity, and air pressure. Some storm chasers have a small radar dish mounted on their vehicle. It probes the sky to help them spot thunderstorms that might produce tornadoes, and then it tracks their movements.

Weather balloons

Each day, weather balloons are released from hundreds of places all over the world. They float up through the atmosphere carrying a small box of instruments called a radiosonde. The radiosonde measures the temperature, air pressure, and humidity, and sends the numbers down to the ground by radio every second or two.

41

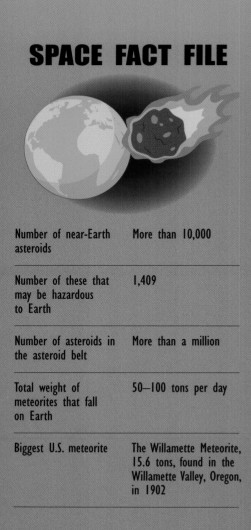

Number of near-Earth asteroids	More than 10,000
Number of these that may be hazardous to Earth	1,409
Number of asteroids in the asteroid belt	More than a million
Total weight of meteorites that fall on Earth	50–100 tons per day
Biggest U.S. meteorite	The Willamette Meteorite, 15.6 tons, found in the Willamette Valley, Oregon, in 1902

Mission control

Manned and unmanned spacecraft scan space for anything that might harm us. They send pictures and data down to control rooms where scientists and engineers monitor these missions.

SPACE HAZARDS

There is weather in space, and it sometimes affects us here on Earth. Space weather near Earth is caused by the Sun. Storms and explosions on the surface of the Sun send out clouds of particles and waves of energy. They usually miss Earth, but sometimes they come straight toward us. When they arrive, they can damage satellites and cause power cuts. Spacecraft constantly watch the Sun to give an early warning of damaging space weather. There are other dangers in space, too. Rocks of all sizes move through space, and sometimes they hit Earth.

Early warning craft

A spacecraft called the Solar and Heliospheric Observatory (SOHO) has been watching the Sun since 1995. Its cameras and other instruments can give up to three days' warning of severe space weather.

The spotty Sun

Dark spots called sunspots sometimes appear on the Sun. They are storms like hurricanes on Earth. When the Sun is more active, it has more sunspots and it's more likely to produce space weather that will affect us here on Earth.

Asteroid strike

Large rocks called asteroids travel through space. Most asteroids stay far away from Earth, but once in a while one of them comes close. One day, a really big asteroid might smash into Earth's surface. Scientists search space for the most dangerous asteroids.

The stormy Sun

The Sun's surface is a stormy, boiling ocean of searing-hot gas. Explosions bigger than the size of Earth send gas and radiation streaming out into space. They cause the space weather that affects us here on Earth.

Nature's light show

An eerie glow is often seen in the sky near the poles. It's caused by particles from the Sun, called the solar wind, diving into the atmosphere and making the air glow. In the north, this glow is called the Northern Lights or aurora borealis. In the south it's called the Southern Lights or aurora australis. Space weather can make this light show bigger and brighter.

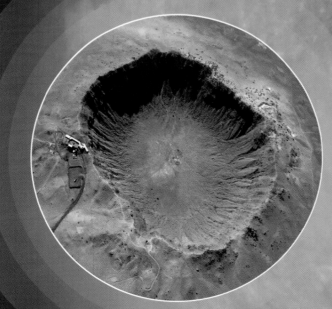

Crater maker

Most of the pieces of rock that enter Earth's atmosphere from space burn up before they reach the ground. Only the biggest rocks survive their journey through the atmosphere and smash into the surface. This crater in Arizona is 4,000 feet across. It was made when a rock 160 feet across hit Earth 50,000 years ago. A space rock that reaches the ground is called a meteorite.

Stars with tails

Occasionally, something that looks like a star with a bright tail appears in the sky. It's a comet. As it nears the Sun, it warms up and gives out gas and dust, which forms the tail. Comets have hit Earth in the past, and might again in the future.

Predictions for Earth in the year 2100 compared to 2000:

Air temperature	3–8.5°F higher
Sea level	3–5 feet higher
Seawater	More acidic
Rainfall	More in some places, less in others
Snow cover	Less
Glaciers	Smaller
Sea ice	Less

Living with volcanoes

People who live near volcanoes have to plan for the future. More than a million people live on the slopes of a volcano called Mount Etna in Sicily. If an eruption is thought likely, there are plans to move them to safety.

THE FUTURE OF OUR PLANET

There are certain to be more natural disasters and wild weather in the future. Most scientists think the world will be warmer and there will be more extreme storms, floods, heat waves, and droughts, but it is so difficult to look into the future that no one really knows what will happen.

Protecting London

London, the capital city of the United Kingdom, is protected from flooding by a barrier across the river Thames. If there is a danger of flooding, gates in the Thames Barrier are closed to keep the sea out.

Disappearing glaciers

Glaciers are rivers of solid ice that slide downhill very slowly. They are made of ice that fell as snow. Then the snow was squashed and changed into ice by more snow falling on top. As the world warms, less snow falls and glaciers also melt faster. The Sheldon Glacier in Antarctica is one of many glaciers that are now shrinking and retreating.

New islands

Volcanoes sometimes erupt under the sea, growing higher and higher with every eruption. In time, they may appear above the waves and form a new island. In 2013 a volcano emerged out of the Pacific Ocean near Japan. It continued erupting and growing bigger until it joined onto a nearby island called Nishinoshima.

Supervolcano

Yellowstone National Park ranges over the states of Wyoming, Montana, and Idaho. It is also the top of a volcano so big that it's called a supervolcano. Yellowstone has erupted three times in the past two million years. No one knows if it will erupt again in the future.

British Isles if all the ice on Earth were to melt.

British Isles today

Sea level rise

Over the past hundred years, the global sea level has risen by 4–8 inches. Most scientists think the sea level will continue to rise, but no one knows how much more it will rise or how fast it will happen. Some low-lying islands and coasts may be flooded, and the people who live there today may have to move away to higher ground.

HOW TO BUILD YOUR VOLCANO

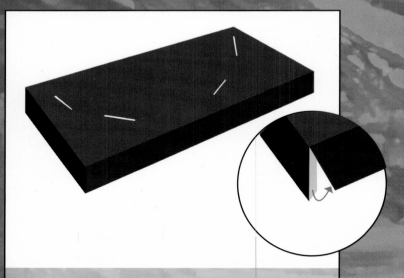

1. Make the first section with the "A" pieces. Fold down the sides of the base and glue tabs to the edges on the inside.

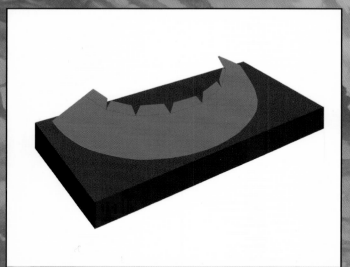

2. Slide the four tabs at the bottom of the volcano's widest section into the slots on top of the base. Turn the piece over and glue the tabs to the underside of the base.

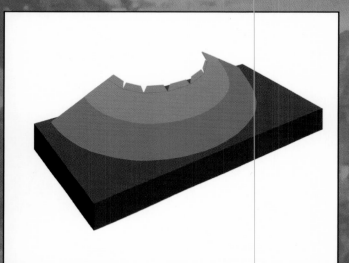

3. Glue the tabs that line the top of the widest section to the underside edge of the volcano's middle section.

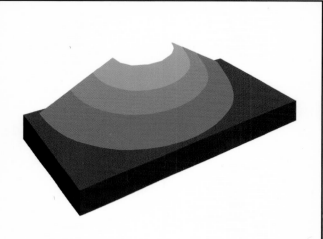

4. Glue the tabs that line the top of the middle section to the underside edge of the volcano's top section.

5. Glue the tabs of the cross section piece to the inner side of the volcano. Repeat steps 1–5 with the "B" pieces to make the other half of the volcano.

6. Connect the halves by pushing the tab at the base of section A into the slot on section B and glue it on the inside. Slot the "eruption" piece at the top of section A.

Ash and gas

VOLCANIC ERUPTION

Ash and gas

Crater

Vent — Magma

Flank — Side vent

Conduit (pipe) — Layers of lava and ash

Magma chamber — Rock layers of Earth's crust

Index